This Book Belongs to :

_____

Scan this QR Code to view more coloring books!

Copyrighted Material

Farm Animals Coloring Book by Nouha Gallery ©
All rights reserved. No part of this book may be used or reproduced in any form without written permission.

Dear Parents

Welcome to the Farm Animals Coloring Book! My name is Nouha, I am an engineer and a visual artist passionate about fun and positive learning environments. I have worked with kids for years and decided to contribute with a collection of books carefully developed to enhance your child's creativity, nurture their curiosity, create memories and teach them with joy.

Children between the age of one to eight have awesome energy we as parents need to channel effectively. The Farm Animals Coloring Book is a great place to start. It can be a "Let's color together" session, where you engage, talk about the day, or simply enjoy a sweet parent-child moment. Or, a solo coloring session, which is profoundly therapeutic and calming.

As children shift their focus to concentrate on finishing their masterpiece, this peaceful activity can provide an outlet for processing emotions and take the focus off challenging situations.

Through these pages, your child will explore, experiment, and learn. Practicing is important to improve fine motor skills, and messy mistakes are crucial and beautiful!

The Farm Animals Coloring Book contains animals your child may come across at farms, iin books, or in documentaries. A page to test colors, and explore choices to improve decision-making skills is attached. All designs are hand-drawn carefully to include different levels of difficulty and purposely made bold for a better coloring experience.

Your child will also explore multiple concepts and ideas through hand-drawn activity pages such as mazes and dot-to-dot, providing more than just fun! A completion certificate is attached at the end of the book to color, cut, and keep!

Positive reviews from wonderful customers like you help other parents feel confident about choosing the Farm Animals Coloring Book. Sharing your happy experience will be greatly appreciated!

I hope you enjoy the Farm Animals Coloring Book! Happy Coloring!

-Nouha.H

 # Color testing
Test your Colors here

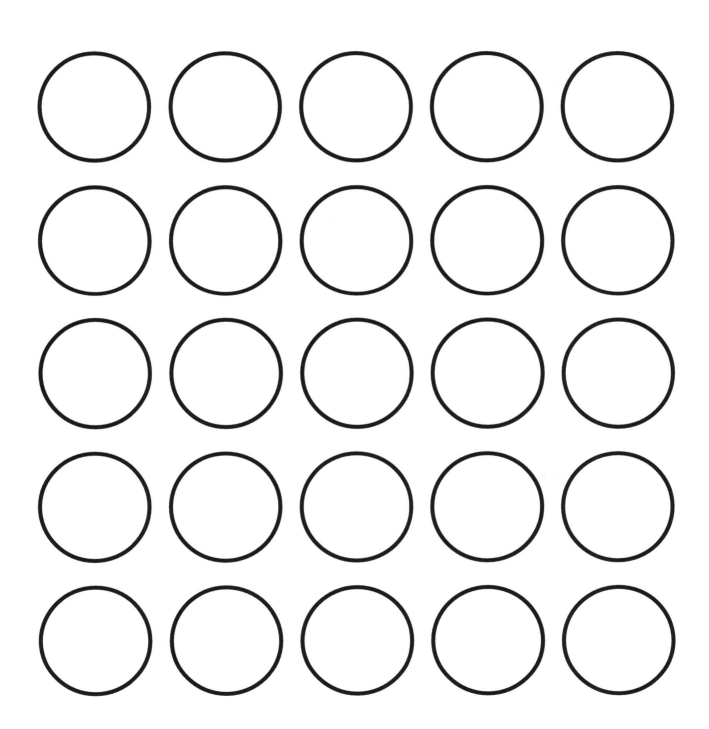

Cows are female cattle. They are large vegetarian mammals. Cows eat grass and produce milk.

Bulls are male cattle. Bulls are much more muscular than cows.

A baby cow is called a "calf". Calves are born with super sharp teeth.

Goats are one of the cleanest animals. They are very intelligent and curious. Goats can be taught their name and to come when called.

Sheep are very gentle and clever animals. They also have an excellent sense of smell. Sheep eat grass and plants.

A "hen" is a female chicken. Hens lay eggs. Most breeds of chickens can fly for short distances.

Baby chickens are called "chicks". Chickens can have up to 12 chicks at a time.

A male chicken is called a "rooster". Roosters are larger and usually more brightly colored compared to chickens.

Ducks have highly waterproof feathers. Ducks' legs are set far back on their bodies, which helps them swim well but makes them waddle when walking.

A Goose is a large bird with loud, honking calls. Geese are generally larger than ducks but smaller than swans. Most geese are black, brown, gray, or white.

Ostrich is the largest living bird. Unlike most birds, the ostrich cannot fly, but can run very fast.

Turkeys are large round birds with dark feathers. They can be very fast whether they are walking or running.

Peacocks are beautiful large birds that can dance and fly!

Dogs have superior hearing compared to humans and a remarkable sense of smell.

Cats have flexible bodies and sharp teeth.
They sleep 13 to 14 hours a day.

Horses are herbivore mammals. They are very smart and can sleep standing up. Horses can't breathe through their mouth.

Donkeys are smaller than horses, and have larger ears. Donkeys are strong, intelligent and have an incredible memory.

A pony is a small horse. Ponies are gentle and strong.

Llamas have elongated faces with banana-sized ears. Llamas are a lot bigger than their cousins the alpacas.

Alpacas have small, blunt faces with short ears and shaggy hair. They are typically shy and polite.

A baby rabbit is called a "kit". Rabbits are very social creatures and live in groups.

Pigs have poor eyesight but a great sense of smell. A baby pig is called a "piglet".

Bees have 5 eyes and 6 legs. Worker bees produce honey from pollen and nectar that they collect from plants.

Pigeons are incredibly intelligent and have excellent hearing abilities. They can hear distant storms and volcanoes.

Other things you can find on a farm !

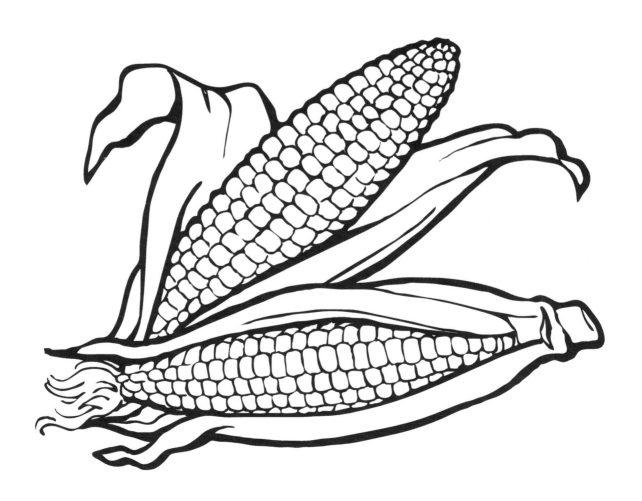

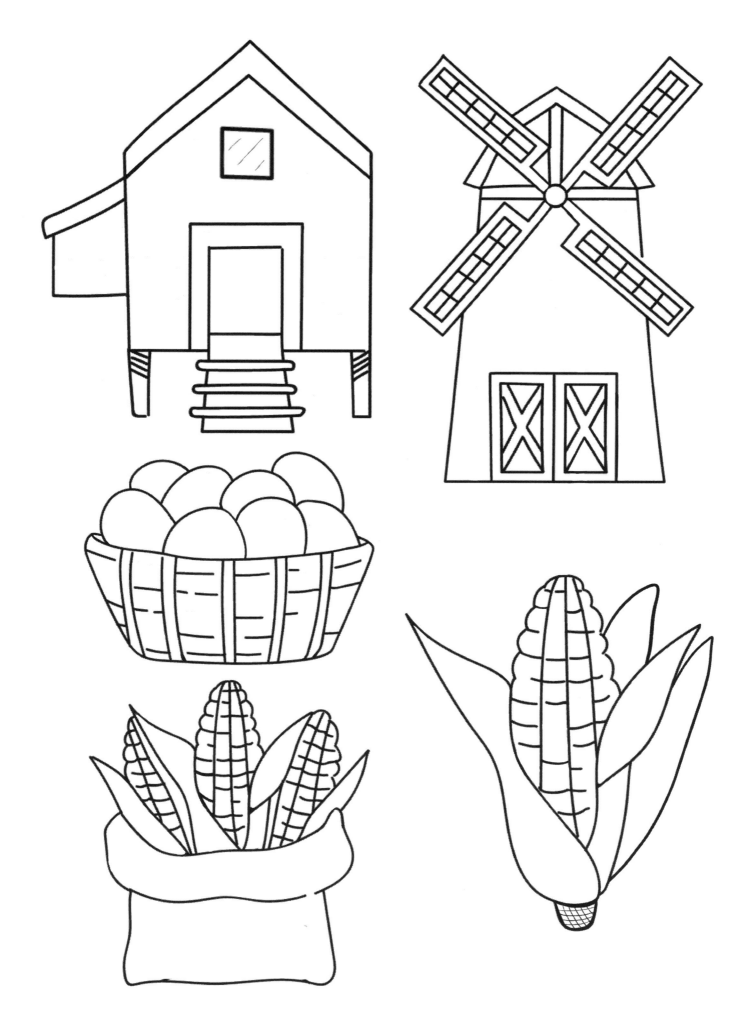

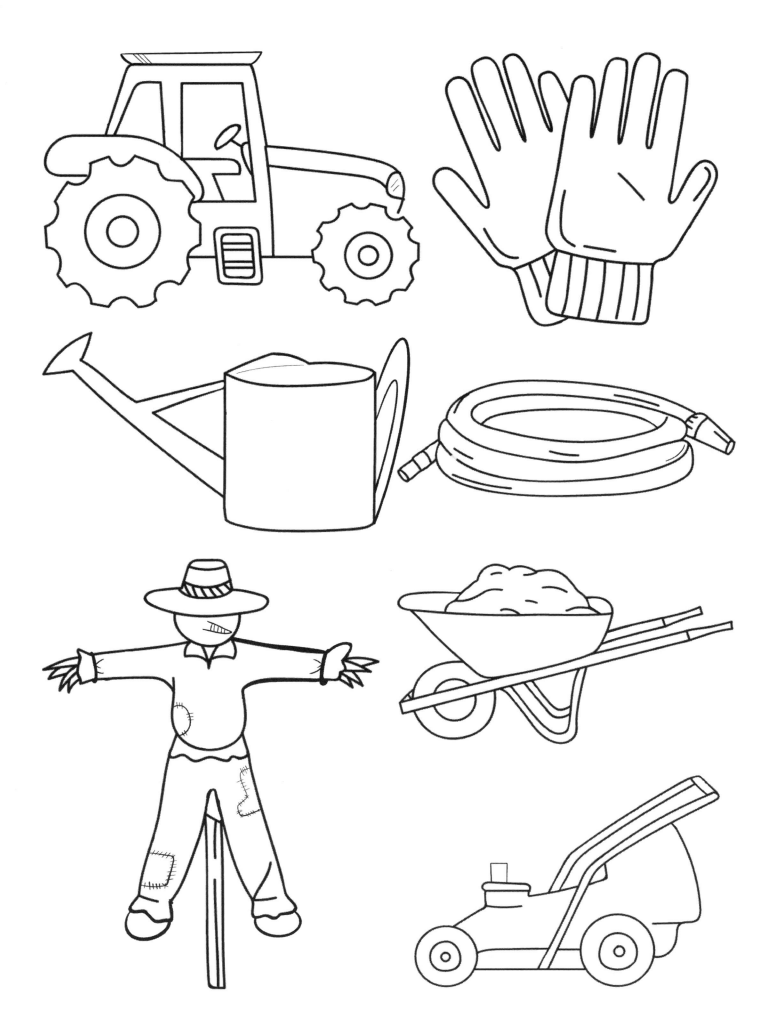

Flowers

Butterfly

Ladybug

Snail

Ant

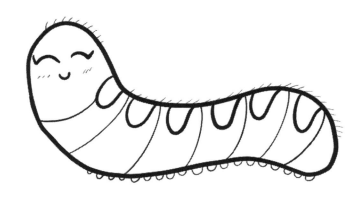

Caterpillar

Beetle

Activity time!

CONNECT THE DOTS

CONNECT THE DOTS

Connect the Dots

You are a-Maze-ing

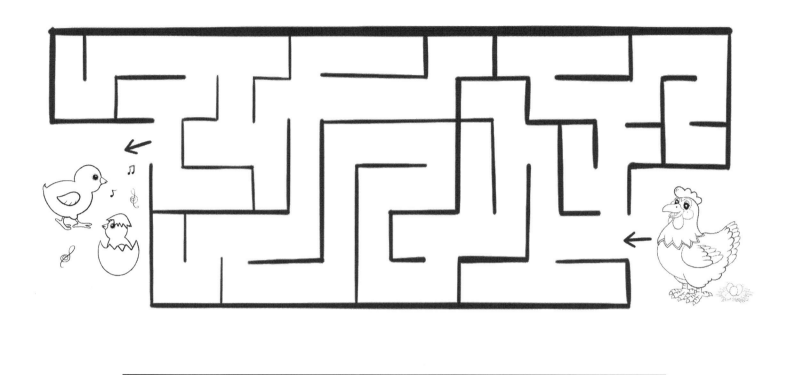

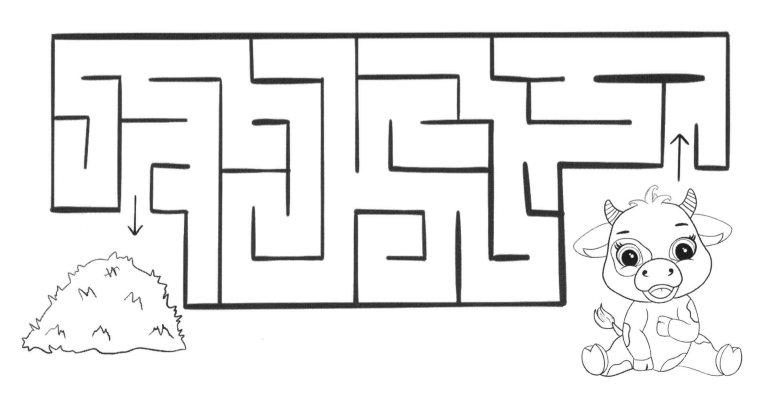

Count and Color

Spot 10 Differences

GUESS THE ANIMAL

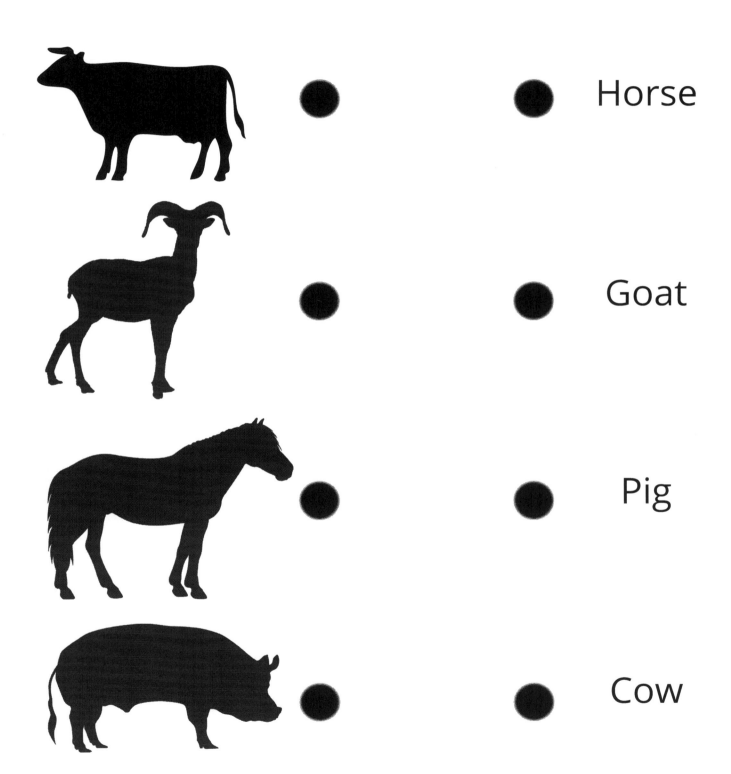

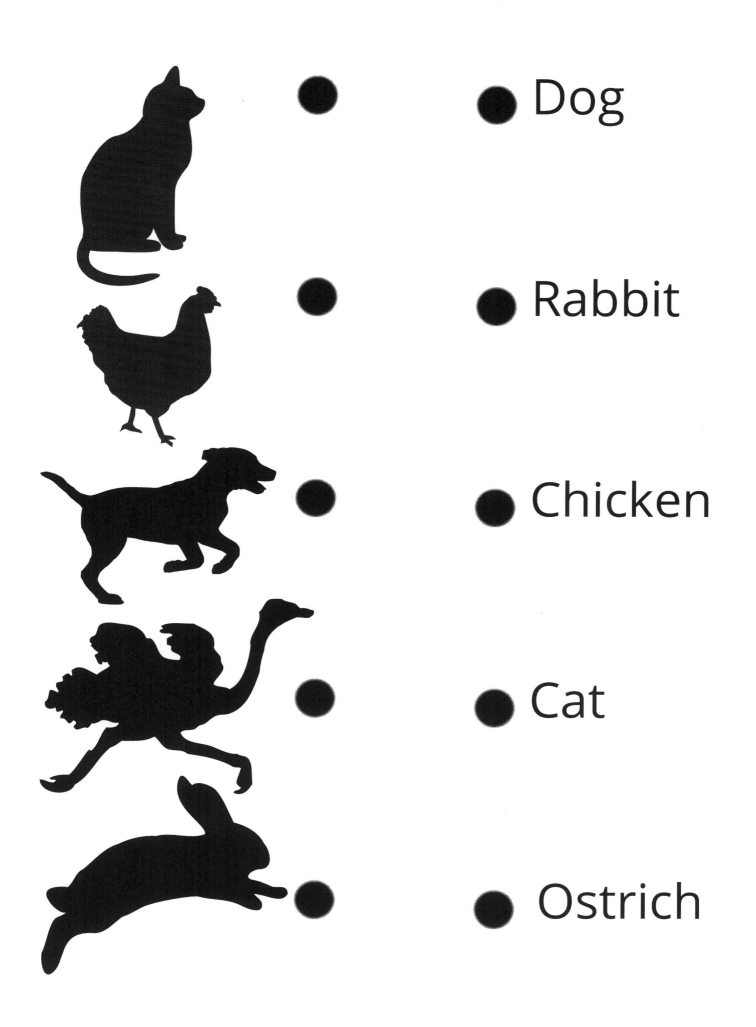

Word Search

```
S P Q O N A Q I B F Y W U L P Z S
J C L S F E E R R J T Z L X E H D
K I S T R L P B O G D N Y O A O O
V X C R N Y E L C P G C O W C R N
K G E I K C D N Q V W C T C O S K
T D U C K D Y X F T I Z S Q C E E
C A T H Z O Q T G H Y N P S K Y Y
Y O F P T G R O O S T E R C V W E
F I L J S N L N W J X Q G O A T Q
E B E E H B T M W U D Y O K O C L
E H P W E B Q U I T C J L L A M A
M F O V E X T E W A L P A C A X C
Y H N F P U O B I R D J J A O L L
C B Y R A B B I T C P H C L A K W
E P L M G L F X T W U P F F T P U
I T R Q A C H I C K E N D Q F N P
V K I H U P A Z U P E V P I G R I
```

PONY, LLAMA, GOAT, COW, RABBIT, OSTRICH, CALF, HORSE, DUCK, PEACOCK, CHICKEN, DOG, SHEEP, DONKEY, ROOSTER, BEE, ALPACA, PIG, CAT, BIRD

Word Search Solution

```
S P Q O N A Q I B F Y W U L P Z S
J C L S F E E R R J T Z L X E H D
K I S T R L P B O G D N Y O A O O
V X C R N Y E L C P G C O W C R N
K G E I K C D N Q V W C T C O S K
T D U C K D Y X F T I Z S Q C E E
C A T H Z O Q T G H Y N P S K Y Y
Y O F P T G R O O S T E R C V W E
F I L J S N L N W J X Q G O A T Q
E B E E H B T M W U D Y O K O C L
E H P W E B Q U I T C J L L A M A
M F O V E X T E W A L P A C A X C
Y H N F P U O B I R D J J A O L L
C B Y R A B B I T C P H C L A K W
E P L M G L F X T W U P F F T P U
I T R Q A C H I C K E N D Q F N P
V K I H U P A Z U P E V P I G R I
```

PONY, LLAMA, GOAT, COW, RABBIT, OSTRICH, CALF, HORSE, DUCK, PEACOCK, CHICKEN, DOG, SHEEP, DONKEY, ROOSTER, BEE, ALPACA, PIG, CAT, BIRD

Farm Animals
Certificate of Completion

Presented to

_____

For Outstanding Performance

Signature
Nouha Gallery

Date
....

Scan me to re-order this book

Made in the USA
Columbia, SC
14 November 2022